ZiGGY'S®
Divine
COMEDY

Ziggy's® Divine Comedy

BY Tom Wilson

**Andrews McMeel
Publishing**

Kansas City

www.uexpress.com and www.andrewsmcmeel.com

98 99 00 01 02 BAH 10 9 8 7 6 5 4 3 2 1

ISBN: 0-8362-6826-1

Library of Congress Catalog Card Number: 98-85356

8

15

...IF YOU ALWAYS EXPECT DISAPPOINTMENT

... YOU WON'T BE DISAPPOINTED!!

...I FINALLY FIGURED OUT WHY I NEVER HAVE ANY MONEY...

...I'M ALWAYS SQUANDERING IT PAYING BILLS!!

19

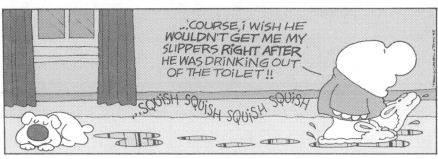

27

28

30

47

50

11-38

63

65

69

91

ZIGGY, i REALIZE THAT THEY ALL DEPEND ON YOU ... BUT THAT DOESN'T QUALIFY YOU TO CLAIM THEM ON YOUR INTERNAL REVENUE FORMS AS "DEPENDENTS"!

NOBODY GOT WHERE THEY ARE TODAY...

BY LIVING IN THE PAST!!

99

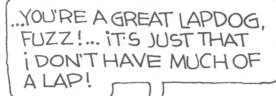